Building the Kingdom through Business

A Mission Strategy for the 21st Century World

Bridget Adams and Manoj Raithatha

instant
apostle

First published in Great Britain in 2012

Instant Apostle
The Hub
3-5 Rickmansworth Road
Watford
Herts
WD18 OGX

British Library Cataloguing-in-Publication Data

A catalogue record for this book is available from the British Library

This book and all other Instant Apostle books are available from Instant Apostle:

Website: www.instantapostle.com
E-mail: info@instantapostle.com

ISBN 978-0-9559135-1-8

Printed in Great Britain

Instant Apostle is a new way of getting ideas flowing, between followers of Jesus, and between those who would like to know more about His Kingdom.

It's not just about books and it's not about a one way information flow. It's about building a community where ideas are exchanged. Ideas will be expressed at an appropriate length. Some will take the form of books. But in many cases ideas can be expressed more briefly than in a book. Short books, or pamphlets, will be an important part of what we provide. As with pamphlets of old, these are likely to be opinionated, and produced quickly so that the community can discuss them.

Well known authors are welcome, but we also welcome new writers. We are looking for prophetic voices, authentic and original ideas, produced at any length; quick and relevant, insightful and opinionated. And as the name implies, these will be released very quickly, either as Kindle books or printed texts or both.

Join the community. Get reading, get writing and get discussing!

Table of Contents

Acknowledgements..1

Foreword by Ram Gidoomal 2

Foreword by Mats Tunehag..5

Introduction 7

Setting the Scene...11

The Kingdom of God is Like... 11

Business Matters!...12

Sacred Secular Divide?...15

Looking Backwards to Move Forward 17

The Quaker Example...19

Business is a Ministry! 21

And We Conclude? 22

The Kingdom, the Bible and Business 25

Good News: Economics or Theology? 25

Some Thoughts Around Work 28

Work, Wealth Creation and Business 30

Some Strange Stories...33

And We Conclude? 35

What is a Kingdom Building Business?....................................37

CSR+ 38

But what is a Spiritual Bottom Line? 40

Business Ethics...43

And We Conclude? 45

Some Examples 47

CSR+ in action 47

Building the Kingdom through...Building! 49

Reshaping Financial Products.......................................51

Blessing the Community with Cheesecake: a Case Study by Mats Tunehag 53

And We Conclude? 55

How Can I Set Up a Kingdom Business?......................56

I Have a Business Idea...What do I do?.........................56

Begin with God 57

Put the Business Idea Down on Paper.....................57

Go Deeper 57

Does this Work? 58

Get Started 59

BAM in a Box...59

Teams Work! 61

Spider or Starfish?...64

Leadership Jesus Style! 67

And We Conclude? 69

And We Conclude FINALLY..71

What They are Saying about Business and the Kingdom.....73

Dr David Landrum, Evangelical Alliance 73

Ram Gidoomal CBE, Chair of Traidcraft.......................74

Jerry Marshall, General Manager of Transformational Business Network (TBN) 74

Transformational SME: Transforming Lives Through Business 75

Charles Hippsley: The London Institute for Contemporary Christianity..76

Terry Diggines: A Call to Business..77

Bridget Adams: WorkPlace Inspired and the Kingdom Business School 78

Proverbs 31:10–31...79

Resource Directory 81

Some Books We Found Helpful...83

Acknowledgements

There are many people whose help we have relied on to produce this book. We want thank Ram Gidoomal and Mats Tunehag for their encouragement, and its expression in the forewords. And a big thank you to Mats for allowing us to use so much of his material. Thanks also to Nigel Sykes for many illuminating discussions on his model of leadership and company growth. And we thank those running the businesses we have highlighted in our case studies; although busy people they made time to help us.

Our designers deserve a mention here. David Salmon, Breath Creative and Steve Hill, Ratio 7, have done us proud and we are grateful.

The UK Evangelical Alliance has been most supportive, and we especially thank Dr David Landrum for his encouragement.

We thank our families, who have patiently waited while we spent long hours preparing this book.

And, of course, to the One who makes it all possible and worthwhile, eternal thanks are due!

Foreword by Ram Gidoomal

It is becoming increasingly evident that a business environment that is devoid of ethics and socially aware decision-making is no longer sustainable.

Consequently, there is an even greater urgency than ever before for business professionals and organisations to engage their consciences and re-examine their attitudes towards financial systems and financial practices with regards to ethics and morality.

The evidence is on the news every day. Inequality has become even more of a problem than it was even half a decade ago, and this has implications for both the rich and poor. This inequality finds its natural expression in the general public's attitudes towards executive pay or financial privilege, and at the more extreme end, the sort of social unrest that seems to be increasing across the globe.

Of course, I am referring to the executive salary question and the Occupy movement at one end of the spectrum, and the Arab Spring on the other end, as well as the sorts of riots that Hackney and Westminster saw last year, although the London rioters were motivated as much by personal greed as social indignation.

Meanwhile, corporate business is increasingly aware that it is impossible to separate personal ethics and values from corporate ethics and values. In other words, corporate greed and corruption will only occur where there is personal greed and corruption. In terms of inequality, statistics have shown that the gap between rich and poor is not just widening in the developing nations, but also in developed nations such as the

UK and the US. A high-level banker recently said we are sitting on a social time bomb, and it's ticking.

Time is running out and we need to be doing something sooner rather than later.

This book by Manoj and Bridget is a timely contribution to a complex issue and offers some useful material to stimulate healthy discussion and debate. The solution depends on our own personal attitudes and where we draw the line for ourselves in terms of personal wealth and business ethics. Mahatma Gandhi said: 'There is enough for every man's need, but not for every man's greed.'

It is obvious to me that we have crossed the line and reached a meltdown of sorts. What we need to do now is find new models of sustainable and ethical business and Manoj and Bridget offer some useful and practical tips and guidelines in this respect.

They give a number of examples of ethical businesses and business practices that benefit all parties including the organisations themselves and those who lead them, the shareholders, the producers and members of their supply chain, and the consumers themselves who are demanding higher degrees of business virtue than ever before.

I am honoured to have been asked to write a foreword to this publication, which is a valuable contribution to a complex and controversial issue.

Ram Gidoomal CBE

Entrepreneur, strategic advisor and former United Kingdom Group chief executive of the Inlaks Group.

Chairman of the Lausanne International board, Traidcraft plc and Traidcraft Exchange, Winning Communications Partnership, South Asian Concern, Allia (Industrial and Provident Society) Ltd, The Office of the Independent Adjudicator for Higher Education, Hendersons Global SRI Advisory Committee

Board Member of the International Justice Mission, an External Member of the Audit and Risk Committee of the UK Equalities and Human Rights Commission, a Council Member of the United Kingdom Evangelical Alliance (UKEA), Advisory Board member of the Institute of Business Ethics

Patron of Employability Forum which helps refugees and asylum seekers to find employment and was a member of the Home Office/UKBA Complaints Audit Committee (2005–2009), trustee of Care for Children and a vice president of The Leprosy Mission and Livability (formerly Shaftesbury Society).

Foreword by Mats Tunehag

This is an important book, almost a pamphlet in the best Clapham group tradition. It is profoundly biblical, historically reflective and immensely practical. Wilberforce and the Clapham group were deeply motivated by profound biblical truths; they understood their times and fought for a systemic change.

Bridget Adams and Manoj Raithatha make important observations on the unbiblical and secular–sacred divide. This notion permeates our thinking and it stifles our ability to 'shape the world for good and for God'.

The book clearly demonstrates a God perspective on work and business, and points out the need for wealth creation – for the common good and God's glory.

Adams and Raithatha align with the growing global Business as Mission movement, but suggest the term Kingdom Building Business. They illustrate the transformational nature of the concept by telling the story of the Quakers, whose guiding light was 'spiritual and solvent'.

God is the original entrepreneur, and throughout His-story we've seen men and women who have made a positive difference through business. *Building the Kingdom through Business* may provoke some, but it will certainly inspire, educate and equip a new generation of Kingdom building business people. But we are not just aiming for a few inspired people and a few more Kingdom building businesses. No, we dream of and work for a paradigm shift – in the Church and in the market place.

This book is an important part to that end.

Mats Tunehag

Global spokesperson on Religious Liberty for the World Evangelical Alliance.

Member of the Global Council of Advocates International, a global network of 30,000 lawyers in over 120 countries.

Senior Associate on Business as Mission for both the Lausanne Movement and for the World Evangelical Alliance Mission Commission.

Introduction

As we sit here, in the calm before the storm of writing, preparing this book together, a thought strikes us. We realise that anyone looking at us would immediately see how different we are. We are different generations, different genders, and different races.

Manoj is a British Asian, who grew up in Watford, but spent a lot of his early years in Kenya too. He is married with small children. He began his career as a teacher before turning to writing. He went on to write a Bafta-award-winning children's TV series 'My Life as a Popat'. In 2003, Manoj turned his hand to business and set up a property company trading in the buying and selling of residential new build apartments across England. But ultimately it was the ill health of his two year old son in 2008 which was to prove the biggest turning point in Manoj's life. Christian friends set up a prayer vigil. Miraculously he was healed and within days Manoj, a born and raised Hindu, found himself giving his life to serve Jesus. Today, Manoj continues to run his business and also heads up the South Asian Forum (SAF), a grouping within the Evangelical Alliance, set up to equip the Church for mission to Asians of other faiths. He recently coordinated the production of the booklet 'Jesus through Asian Eyes', which is being used by many churches in the UK, and beyond.

Bridget has traced her family tree back as far as the 14th century in England. She grew up in Windsor, and is widowed with a brood of grown up children and grandchildren. She started as a physicist in university and government laboratories before moving into the hi-tech business sector. In business she worked in sales, marketing and general management, up to director level. Although brought up as a Christian, she only reconnected with her faith in her forties. She was amazed to find that God was calling her into the ordained ministry of the Church of England and resisted the call for some years! It was only when she was obedient and put herself forward for selection, was chosen for training and came out the other side of the process that she realised that God was not calling her into parish work but into priesthood in the business world. Although slow on the uptake, she now works to develop and network Christian-run businesses, and runs WorkPlace Inspired.

Anyone looking at us must think what on earth do these two people have in common? Although they may not see it, we are brother and sister! Not naturally, but supernaturally. Our journeys have been different, but our end point is the same; Jesus. We are both citizens of the Kingdom where all those differences melt away. We have been to the cross; we know the love of God and have been transformed in the fire of it, a fire that forges us together. And a fire that now burns in our hearts for the people around us. We love the King and we share a passion to work with Him to help build His Kingdom; on earth as it is in heaven.

Yes we are both citizens of that Kingdom here and now, but we continue to live in this world too. And the world is a dark place at the moment; the veneer of civilisation wears thin in places. Our news media are filled with stories about terrorism, the credit crunch, rising unemployment, natural disasters, crime, breakdown of communities and breakdown of families. We see violence, selfishness and lack of compassion. In today's world many live in fear. Many have lost hope. Is it any wonder our young people are running riot? As people who have found hope, meaning and purpose through Jesus, we ache when we look at the world around us that is drowning in a sea of hopelessness, meaninglessness and lack of purpose.

We are part of the Church that has a mission, from the Latin *missio*, or sending. The pattern is set in chapter 20 of John's Gospel. Immediately after the resurrection, the fledgling Church receives the Spirit Jesus, who then instructs them; 'As the Father has sent me, I am sending you'. We are sent. Just as those first Christians were, we are sent into the alien culture around us. We are sent with a message of love, and we are sent to bring transformation to individuals and to communities.

But it's not easy to get that message heard, let alone accepted. Not only is the culture we are sent to alien, it is also rapidly changing. It seems to change faster than we can respond to it. We need new answers, but we are faced with a blank page each time we try to frame a response. We are thinking on our feet. This is no bad thing; it was true for the apostolic Church and yet that was a time of great growth. In his letters we see Paul as a dynamic improviser, grappling with topics for which there were no set answers. That is not to say that he was making it up as he went along. He had the resource of the Jewish Scriptures and he had firsthand knowledge of Jesus that he used to find the answers to new questions that were being asked by Christians of different races, languages and backgrounds. We have those resources too, plus the writings and experiences of generations of Christians.

In this book we want to start writing on some of the pages that are blank for our generation. We want to share our ideas and experience of being and telling good news through business. What does it mean to be sent to the world in and through business? What does it mean for those who are sent, what does it mean for the Church and what does it mean for the Kingdom of God?

Instant Apostle, the publisher for this book, is a business that we have set up together, and which embodies the principles we are writing about. It is a cooperative venture, a community of authors and readers where everyone is treated fairly and with respect. All communication is open and transparent; there are no hidden agendas. And it provides a platform for new voices, new ideas, which can help to shape the world for good and for God. Our hope is that it is a Kingdom building business. If you like this book, then why not try another from Instant Apostle!

Setting the Scene

The Kingdom of God is Like...

In May 1944 an American Judge gave a speech in Central Park, New York. To a country then at war, he spoke about the spirit of liberty. He said:

What then is the spirit of liberty? I cannot define it; I can only tell you my own faith. The spirit of liberty is the spirit which is not too sure that it is right; the spirit of liberty is the spirit which seeks to understand the minds of other men and women; the spirit of liberty is the spirit which weighs their interests alongside its own without bias; the spirit of liberty remembers that not even a sparrow falls to earth unheeded; the spirit of liberty is the spirit of Him who, near two thousand years ago, taught mankind that lesson it has never learned, but has never quite forgotten; that there may be a kingdom where the least shall be heard and considered side by side with the greatest.

Like Judge Learned Hand, we find that we cannot quite define liberty or quite define the Kingdom either, but we know that they go hand in hand. In this quotation there is something of the real essence of both. And of Jesus, whose Kingdom it is. Jesus declared that He had come to bring freedom, saying 'you will know the truth, and the truth will set you free'. And He told many stories about the Kingdom of

God, or the Kingdom of heaven, which is the same. It is the Kingdom of the truly free. The stories Jesus told don't define the Kingdom, but each gives us an idea of the flavour of it. The Kingdom is where the best thing that you can be is like a child; it's where we forgive each other because we are forgiven by God; it's where everyone, good and bad, rich and poor, is invited to a great banquet arranged by a king. It's where God's will is done, on earth as it is in heaven. And God's will has always been for justice and against exploitation.

This strange, attractive Kingdom grows in a way we cannot explain. It's like yeast mixed into flour, changing the flour completely. Or it's like a tiny seed that is planted...and then grows into an enormous tree! It's organic. Jesus said, 'The coming of the kingdom of God is not something that can be observed, nor will people say, "Here it is" or "There it is", because the kingdom of God is in your midst.'

As Learned Hand asserts, there is a resonance in the world with the idea of the Kingdom. It is something people yearn for without even knowing what it is. The Kingdom is recognised when it's seen, and missed when it isn't seen. When we discover how to see it in our midst, we can help other people to see it too, to choose it and to work alongside God, and us, to increase the Kingdom on earth.

And with that in mind, we start thinking about business and the Kingdom.

Business Matters!

In his book *Screw Business as Usual*, Sir Richard Branson outlines his vision for nothing less than global transformation. He asks, 'Can we bring more meaning to our lives and help change the world at the same time...a whole new way of doing things, solving major problems and turning our work into something we both love and are proud of.' His proposed solution is a new way of doing business. 'It is time to...shift our values, to switch from a profit focus to caring for people, communities and the planet.' Sometimes God uses prophets from outside the Church!

The world, it seems, wants business to change. The voices, powerful voices, are being heard out there. The Church, who you might think would be driving this new found hunger for ethics and transformative business, is in danger of being left behind. Branson knows that business can change the world for good, but we believe it can also change the world for God. Business can help build the Kingdom.

Business matters, because business has clout. Broadly, and perhaps crudely, speaking, in the pre-modern period the Church shaped society, in the modern period the nation state shaped it and in the contemporary, or post-modern, world society is shaped by businesses. And they shape it across the whole world, operating across national borders in globalised markets. To call this world dominated by products and services a consumer society, or a consumer driven society, is not strictly accurate. The Marxist post-modern prophet Jean Baudrillard and others have pointed out that in this new scenario it is not consumer needs that drive the markets, but rather the corporations that control consumer behaviour by generating wants that are then perceived as needs. He writes, 'we must agree with Galbraith and others in acknowledging that the liberty and sovereignty of the consumer are nothing more than a mystification'. Buying products indicates buying into a lifestyle; indoctrination of consumers relies on generating aspirations to this lifestyle. The economy relies on creating ever expanding human wants in order to maintain growth. In this brave new world brand awareness is key. The logo is a totem, or symbol uniting the 'clan' of people who associate themselves with that product range. A recent survey

13

of about 7,000 people in the UK, Germany, Australia, India and Japan, found that more people could identify the golden arches of the McDonald's logo than could identify the Christian cross.

By the end of the last century, neo-liberalism, where market forces are given precedence over all other considerations, had created a society where economics had replaced science, which the century before had replaced theology, as the main way in which society attempts to explain the world. From Church to nation to business; from theology to science to economics. Our world has changed and it is no longer taken for granted that the institution of the Church can shape the world around it directly. But the people who make up the Church can still live out the mission given by Jesus to be salt and light in our communities, bringing flavour and vision. Because people haven't changed, their need for God hasn't changed and God's plan hasn't changed.

If it is business that shapes the world, then why can't the Church work in and through business to shape the world for good and for God? Shaping it for good brings wealth creation in communities, with greater justice and relief from poverty for the world's poor, with the dignity of useful labour. Shaping it for God brings 'life in its fullness', a life reconnected with the One who made us and loves us, bringing hope and meaning and purpose. All of that is good news and is the motivation for Kingdom building businesses.

In October 2009 one of us joined 29 other people at Wheaton College, near Chicago. Christian theologians, business leaders, financiers and church leaders from across the world took part in a global consultation on business and the Church, discussing the opportunities for mission that come from bringing the two together. During that week we generated the Wheaton Declaration on Business as Integral Calling. It refers to the 'sacred calling of a life in business' and asks the Church to consider how it might encourage and support Christian business people to live out this calling. And it concludes:

> It is our deep conviction that businesses that function in alignment with the core values of the Kingdom of God are playing and increasingly should play an important role in holistic transformation of individuals, communities and societies.

Business really does matter to God!

Sacred Secular Divide?

So why have we thought that it doesn't? I remember some years ago seeing a church drama. At the end of the sketch the cast walked to the back of the church, as if leaving at the end of the service. They turned at the door and all waved, 'goodbye God, see you again next week'. It was funny because it felt true for so many of us. We came on Sunday to meet with God, and then left Him there in church while we went back out into the world.

Why do we act as if God is interested in what happens in church but not in what happens in His world? It has become so much a mindset among God's people that it even has a name; the sacred secular divide. We assume that God is interested in what we define as sacred, but not in what we define as secular. Over the years many ideas and trends have fed this divide. There's St Augustine's neo-Platonism, the Greek thinking that places the spiritual over the material, which has fed into our theology. There's the Enlightenment, one result of which was the taking of the public sphere for science so that God was pushed to the sidelines. And then there's the present day outworking of that, where secular humanism has to all intents and purposes become the official religion of our country. Our society tells us that Christianity is allowed within the confines of church buildings but that we have to live by different rules out in the world.

These have all fed the sacred secular divide. But I believe its source lies somewhere else. You see, it's been around for a long time. Hundreds of years before Plato, God and His people had a dialogue through the prophet Isaiah. It's documented in Isaiah 58. The people ask God to support them:

'Why have we fasted,' they say, and you have not seen it? 'Why have we humbled ourselves, and you have not noticed?' Yet on the day of your fasting, you do as you please and exploit all your workers.

And God goes on to tell the people that it's not 'religious activity' He expects from them but a whole life which lives out His principles. The people of Israel and Judah had generated their own sacred secular divide! It seems that fallen human beings find it easier to compartmentalise things. Even when we come to God we put what we are prepared to offer to Him in a compartment; we're not going to let Him have the whole lot! We want to stay in control of our lives, and to do that it's more comfortable to set limits. And like the people that Isaiah was talking to, we can do this by 'doing religion' on one day of the week and living how we choose to the rest of the time. He can have the sacred but we'll keep control of the secular, and we'll define which is which.

In 1992 Malcolm Grundy wrote a book called the *Unholy Conspiracy*. He writes about the scandal of the separation of Church and industry. Both sides conspire to keep Church and business in separate spheres. Religious individualism that came out of the Reformation, later reinforced by Adam Smith's theories, cut economics and theology into two distinct 'kingdoms'. The great reformers like Shaftsbury and Wilberforce were motivated by personal faith, but by and large, as Grundy notes in his opening sentence, 'the churches and industries of Britain occupy separate worlds'. For the most part they seem happy with that separation. Grundy notes the Church's awkwardness about money and adds that it is as if 'one whole section of God's creation is regarded as almost beyond the redemptive process'. We will come back to this later. We simply note now that by and large, the Church has failed to have an impact on business because it considers it beyond the pale, that is, outside its home territory.

But the Bible makes clear that God does not compartmentalise His creation. He is interested in everything, His presence fills everywhere. God is interested in our businesses; are we interested in having Him there? Have we handed it all over to Him, or are we holding something back for ourselves? We have to brave the discomfort of an undivided universe if we truly want to be God's people.

Looking Backwards to Move Forward

Sometimes God shows us new strategies to spread the good news. And sometimes He reminds us of old ones! What can we learn from our history? The first thing we can learn is that there the unholy conspiracy did not always exist. In its early

17

days Christianity spread along the trade routes, both east and west from Jerusalem. Business has been used to help build the Kingdom since the Acts of the Apostles. St Paul's journeys were along the trade routes around the Western end of the Mediterranean. It wasn't just that travel was easier for 'missionaries' along the trade routes. The traders themselves were missionaries, gossiping the gospel as they traded their goods. Paul, of course, was famously in the business of tent making. Merchants were so often missionaries as well that in the early Asian church, the Syriac word for 'merchant' was used as a metaphor for evangelist. And these missionaries used their trade to bring good news, as well as telling good news. One example we found reported was from Vietnam, where a Persian monk in Hanoi in the 8th century, ministered, in part, by assisting in developing trade with China.

But what about closer to home? Although St Augustine is sometimes called the 'Apostle to the English', it is well known that Christianity had reached our shores long before he did in the 6th century. The Romans arrived in England before Christianity became the official religion of Rome in the 4th century. However, Christianity flourished through the Roman trade routes, and there was a thriving Christian community here during most of the Roman occupation. Indeed Christians were persecuted in England under the Romans; our own first recorded martyr Alban died under a Roman sword at the beginning of the 3rd century.

In medieval times the craftsmen and traders in this country were still playing a part in spreading the gospel. In England the livery companies and trade guilds probably had their origins before 1066; it is recorded that the Royal Charter was granted to the Weavers' Company in 1155. The guilds set standards, regulated trade and arbitrated in disputes between members. They provided almshouses and care for those in their trade who were in need, and they provided spiritual care through links with the Church. And it was the guilds that produced The Passion Plays of England, which are some of the oldest pieces of English literature. These plays were performed on the streets of our medieval cities on Church Feast Days, usually on the back of a cart. These performances are sometimes called Mystery Plays; the Latin *misterium* means craft or professional skill. In York, for example, where the plays date back to the 14th century or earlier, each craft guild or 'mysterie' would perform its own play as part of an agreed cycle which would take a full day to view at various stations throughout the city. Yes, 700 years ago there was Christian drama on the streets of our towns and cities and it was the business people who put it there!

Once we get to the era of the Industrial Revolution, then we really need to turn our attention to the Quakers, who pioneered so much of what is important in business today.

The Quaker Example

True godliness don't turn men out of the world but enables them to live better in it and excites their endeavours to mend it. William Penn, *No Cross No Crown,* 1682

When we think of Christians in business in the UK, the Quakers spring readily to mind. Or at least they should do! William Penn, quoted above and himself a businessman, was a friend and colleague of George Fox, the founder of the Society of Friends, and wrote down much of the original theology of the new sect. He went on to become the founder and 'absolute proprietor' of the Province of Pennsylvania, where he planned the city of Philadelphia, or brotherly love. Fox's teachings, as explained by Penn, have motivated many Quakers to try to make the world a better place through business. This was the Business as Mission of the 17th to 20th centuries!

And these were big businesses with a big impact. The names of Cadbury, Fry, Rowntree, Bryant and May, Clark, Wedgwood, Barclay and Lloyd are still household names in the 21st century. But there are also forgotten names. Abraham Darby was an innovative genius in the early 18th century, whose metal working companies were instrumental in starting the Industrial Revolution. A century later the Pease family started and ran the Stockton and Darlington Railway Company, originally set up to transport coal from their mines but later introducing the world's first passenger train. Quaker enterprises formed the basis of British Steel (now Corus) and British Rail, as well as Unilever and ICI.

The Quaker ethics of honesty, hard work and responsibility for others produced businesses that thrived, leaving a legacy and positive example for business ethics through the centuries since. As Joseph Rowntree's biographer notes, 'His father could see nothing incongruous in mentioning his stocks of sugar and the Holy Spirit in the same paragraph of a letter, and it would never have occurred to Joseph that there might be a code of ethics applicable only to commerce'.

Rowntree provides a good example of Quaker social action in a business context. As his company grew, so he consistently implemented social provision and care that preceded what the State would legislate for years later. In 1891 he engaged his first welfare worker, and by 1904 the company had seven welfare workers, almost as many as it had department heads. Rowntree employed his first company doctor and dentist in 1904, offering services free of charge to employees, and a company pension scheme was established in 1906. Paid holiday was introduced in 1918. The company had an extensive programme of social activities and a company newsletter, as well as classes and a library. Rowntree made efforts to make the workplace pleasant and interesting, hoping that men and women could be encouraged, 'to develop all that is best and worthy in themselves'. Like the Cadbury brothers,

Rowntree embarked on a social housing programme to provide accommodation for his employees and for others in need.

Quakers were a persecuted minority, never more than 1% of the population, and not allowed to hold public office until the 19th century. But none the less they used business to transform and shape the UK. They were innovative risk takers in business, and Quaker run businesses networked and worked together, with ideas as well as finance running round the network. Joseph Rowntree was a director of the Midlands and York Railway. The Lloyds and Frys were also actively involved in building railways. Quaker banks and Quaker investors supported Quaker entrepreneurs, but they also worked with them. Demonstrating integrity and trustworthiness to those who were suspicious of Quakers, they were also transparent with each other, opening their books to fellow Quakers.

I find the story of Quaker businesses very encouraging. In terms of their spiritual impact, the social reforms they spearheaded led many to become Christians, if not Quakers, and even today, when they are talked of in glowing terms by a world hungry again for ethics in business, they get Jesus a good press! When it comes to 21st century Christian entrepreneurial businesses we needn't worry about how few we are, just how well we do what God has entrusted us to do and how well we work with each other. We can have an impact!

Business is a Ministry!

Hopefully by now you will agree with us that business can be a ministry and those involved in it can be ministers! There are those who are called as business people, just as there are those who are called as pastors.

When I became a priest, I found it strange that people would come up to me and say 'I'm so pleased God has called you into the ministry'. I was already in 'the ministry', because it is the ministry of all believers. And it's a ministry which is largely outside church buildings. Mark Greene, now based at the London Institute for Contemporary Christianity, has been speaking and writing eloquently about this for years. In his book *Thank God it's Monday* he suggests that church leaders might be 'inadvertently equipping us to support their ministry rather than equipping us to do the work of ours'. It's not just business people who suffer under this system. The whole missionary force of the Church in the working world is by and large waiting to be released. Church congregations may pray for their Sunday School teachers...but not for those who teach in class rooms every day of the week. We may pray for overseas missionaries...but not for the business people who have a very real mission in this country and abroad. We all need prayer and support for our ministries!

Mark Greene refers to an 'unholy hierarchy' of callings (to set alongside the unholy conspiracy!). In this hierarchy it is 'clear' to us churchgoers that the highest calling is as a pastor, followed by an overseas missionary, followed by a charity worker. Medical workers and teachers may make it onto the list somewhere near the bottom, but business people don't make it at all! If we're to help change the world then all this unholy thinking has to stop.

And We Conclude?

When I asked local Indonesian believers how it came to pass that Islam captured most of the population while European

22

missionaries had so little effect, they answered that the Europeans came as missionaries, acted like missionaries, and only left the mission compound to do evangelistic 'raids' into the countryside. The Muslims, in stark contrast, were not missionaries but rather traders and business people who lived among the nationals, held commerce with them, and in the course of their enterprise shared the 'truth' of Islam. (Lausanne Paper on Business as Mission 2004)

One of us had a vision. In it I was walking down a straight road. I knew that the road is the truth. At the end of the road, it forks. I asked God which branch to take. He said neither. 'Keep straight on the pathway between the two roads'. God is calling us to stay in Him. I asked what do the two roads that I saw signify? He said, they represent all the people that we as the Church need to bring in to the truth. And how do we do this I asked? I felt God saying think laterally, think out of the box. If it has been difficult to encourage people into the Church, we need to go out there, get alongside them, and bring Jesus to them. It worked in Indonesia. It can work here!

As long ago as 1945, the report 'Towards the Conversion of England' concluded: 'We are convinced that England will never be converted until the laity use the opportunities for evangelism daily afforded by their various occupations, crafts and professions.'

The Church needs to re-think its relationship with business. It used to be the great medieval Church that influenced society. Today it is business. Business shapes us. Social media shape us; advertising by the big brands shapes us. Business influences what we wear, eat and think. Our aspirations have been shaped by business. Business has got us out of the church and into the high street and into the shops! We as the Church need to rethink our strategy. We have examples from the past. We need to stop the Unholy Conspiracy and realise that business is powerful and it can be good! We can use business to build the Kingdom and bring people to the knowledge and love of Jesus. Business can be part of a mission strategy for the 21st century. Building the Kingdom through business is business as mission.

If you are in leadership in a church that wants to link into the world through its own business or through the businesses of the church members, then this resource is for you! If you already run a business but want to see more of a Kingdom impact, then this resource is for you. If you feel that God is calling you to start a business to help His Kingdom grow, then this resource is for you. Or maybe you are none of the above. Read the book anyway to see what God says to you through it!

The Kingdom, the Bible and Business

What does it mean to build the Kingdom? Many of us pray every day 'Your Kingdom come', adding 'Your will be done on earth, as it is in heaven.' And in that we remind ourselves that the Kingdom coming has something to do with the people of planet earth following God's agenda rather than our own. The Kingdom is where the King is acknowledged as king. And whereas one day every eye will see Him and every knee bow, in the here and now the Kingdom grows as rebels become loyal subjects, and the Kingdom values of love and justice and mercy are set loose in towns and countries and continents.

So, how can business help with that? Read on and find out about the value of our work, how we can work hand in hand with God in His great mission and how we can be good news through wealth creation.

Good News: Economics or Theology?

We have a gospel to proclaim. Good news for all people. But is this good news about economics or theology? There seems to be a gulf between the two disciplines. American commentator Susan Lee, who is both an economist and theologian, has tried to build a bridge between the spheres. At a 2010 conference she shared a stage with the Archbishop of Canterbury, and explained:

Economists are interested in how to make the pie larger.
Theologians are interested in how to divide the pie. And so
many theologians treat capitalism like a Chinese menu. They
pick the wealth-distribution parts and discard the wealth-
creation parts. They assume there can be: work without
incentives, enterprise without income inequality, investment
without market-rates of return. But picking and choosing
isn't an option. Capitalism is an integrated system. And it's
this integration that creates the <u>wealth-making, which is the</u>
<u>basis for wealth-sharing.</u>

This lack of integration has been true for the most part in
our experience; it's all rolled in with the sacred secular divide.
We assume that God is interested in what we see as the
worthy task of wealth distribution but not in the 'unworthy'
task of wealth creation. Of course distribution matters; we
want to see a fair and just society. <u>But profit is not a dirty</u>
<u>word. Profit is what there is to be shared.</u>

The Pope said in his New Year message at the beginning of
2009:

...the illusion that a policy of mere redistribution of existing
wealth can definitively resolve the problem must be set aside.
In a modern economy, the value of assets is utterly dependent
on the capacity to generate revenue in the present and the
future. Wealth creation therefore becomes an inescapable duty,
which must be kept in mind if the fight against material
poverty is to be effective in the long term.

Good distribution is necessary but not sufficient; there must
also be something to distribute. Wealth creation is necessary
but not sufficient; it must be for the common good. We need to
be able to think of both sides of the coin. As London based city
lawyer James Featherby writes in *The White Swan Formula,*

'Good business will not answer the world's problems, but we will struggle to solve the problems of the world without it.'

All three commentators that have been quoted here agree on one thing; ethical business is the way forward. Ethical business will lead to the creation of wealth that will then be distributed fairly. A major problem we see across the world at the moment is that the pie is most definitely getting smaller, and no matter how we cut the pie it is the poor who suffer first, and suffer most. What would be good news for these people?

Each country has its own cultural heritage and baggage. For example, here in the UK the 'battle of St Paul's' in 2011 highlighted quite a few things. As protesters camped outside the London cathedral to protest about the ethics of the nearby banks, one thing that became clear is that the Church isn't very good at talking about money. I have a feeling that this is worse in England than in other countries because our cultural background tells us its vulgar to talk about money, and that being 'in trade' is not quite respectable.

Maybe we should read our Bibles more. Jesus talked more about money than He did about anything other than the Kingdom. And not only that, horror of horrors, He was in trade Himself! Jesus ran a carpentry business for many years of His life. And He chose disciples who were also in trade. The fishermen were not hired hands; they had their own boats and nets, and hired other people. In fact, they were business people. And St Paul, after whom the cathedral is named, was a business man. And Lydia, the first Christian in Europe, was a business woman...and the list goes on. So when 'the Church' tries to speak out about money and commerce and chooses people who are respectable clerics or academics to do so, it is being terribly English but it's also sort of missing the point.

According to Luke, Jesus started his public ministry by reading from Isaiah:

The Spirit of the Lord is upon me, because he has anointed me to bring good news to the poor. He has sent me to proclaim release to the captives and recovery of sight to the blind, to let the oppressed go free, to proclaim the year of the Lord's favour.

Good news for the poor is multifaceted. It's about healing and freedom and the joy of the Lord. It's about just rather than unjust systems. But I suspect that it should also include release from poverty; it is economics as well as theology. And ethical business, Kingdom building business, can do that. It can add not just money in the form of a hand out, but good employment, allowing sustainable growth and human flourishing through dignified labour. Work can be part of the good news too.

Some Thoughts Around Work

If I say work to you, what do you think? What words spring to mind when you think of work? Having asked many people that question over the past few years, there seem to be two distinct types of answer, positive and negative, often from the same people! Work is satisfying, gives a sense of achievement, brings colleagues alongside us and it pays. But work is also frustrating, it's hard, it can be unrewarding and bullying and exploitation are often rife in workplaces. There's good and bad; and there's even a linguistic tension. Vocation sounds good while toil sounds bad!

Well I would like to persuade you that the tension that surrounds work is a theological tension. And once we understand this then I think that we can see that work is a blessing which has been cursed. But which can become a blessing again!

The first part of the tension, the good part, comes from the fact that we are made in the image of a God who works. We only have to get five words into the Bible to find God working. And His work is creation. Later Bible passages refer to creation as the 'work of his hands' (for example Job 34:19, Psalm 8:6, Psalm 19:1, Isaiah 5:12 among others). This is an idea that would have appalled the ancient Greeks! Mount Olympus was a work free zone. Gods didn't work and so educated Greeks tried to avoid it too. Our ideas of God are different, and that shapes our ideas about work. Not only that, but Genesis 1 also tells us that each day God looked at the work He had done and saw that it was good. Our God has job satisfaction. And we are made in His image; we are made to work and we are made to have job satisfaction.

But that's before Genesis 3, where it all falls apart. Adam and Eve turn their backs on God. And a change in their relationship to work is one of the things which is mentioned specifically as a result of that. In verse 17 God says to Adam, 'Cursed is the ground because of you; through painful toil you will eat of it all the days of your life'. See that linguistic flip? Work becomes toil. So through the Fall people are cut off from their work.

But the Old Testament prophets looked forward to the day when we would be reconnected. Isaiah writes of the time when God's people:

> ...will build houses and dwell in them; they will plant vineyards and eat their fruit. No longer will they build houses and others live in them, or plant and others eat. For as the days of a tree, so will be the days of my people; my chosen ones will long enjoy the works of their hands. They will not toil in vain... Isaiah 65:22–23

Notice that linguistic reverse flip in the final two sentences! Isaiah is saying that the curse will be taken away and work will be redeemed. And justice around work will be restored.

Come to the New Testament and we see just how everything is redeemed and restored. What is broken is mended, through Jesus. And our work becomes cooperation with God's work through the Holy Spirit, which ties us close to Him. But, we live in the now and the not yet. The Kingdom is here, but not in its fullness. So, sadly, we can still expect to feel the tension around work. We are fallen people, working alongside other fallen people in fallen systems. But the closer we get to our Redeemer, the more redeemed our work becomes. As St Paul writes, 'Whatever you do, work at it with all your heart, as working for the Lord, not for men, since you know that you will receive an inheritance from the Lord as a reward. It is the Lord Christ you are serving.' (Colossians 3:23–24)

In the secular world people talk about the dignity of labour. We can help them to understand why there is a flourishing through work that can never be achieved through living on handouts. It's what we were created to do!

Work, Wealth Creation and Business

We were put in the garden to be gardeners. And the work of gardening was to make the garden prosper and grow in a way that it couldn't without human intervention. We're told that 'no shrub had yet appeared on the earth and no plant had yet sprung up, for the LORD God had not sent rain on the earth and there was no one to work the ground'. (Genesis 2:5) Human work was to lead to wealth creation, even in the garden.

Despite putting aside our reservations in order to talk about money, perhaps we are right to be careful when talking about the Bible and wealth creation. Sometimes I hear texts quoted out of context and flinch. David Miller, executive director of the Princeton University Faith and Work Initiative, has written about three positions Bible-believing Christians have taken on the issue of wealth. He writes about wealth being considered an offence, an obstacle or an outcome of faith. And probably we could think quite quickly of texts we could snatch to support each of these points of view! Should we reject the material world altogether, and all become ascetics? Should we worry that if we do make some money it will distract us from God? Or do we go the prosperity route and proclaim that God loves us and He wants us to have it all? Somehow we need to come to a more holistic biblical understanding, remembering to bear in mind all the baggage of the sacred secular divide when asking ourselves what God really thinks about money. We can over spiritualise things.

So the first thing I want to suggest is that God is not indifferent to our material needs. He is the God of this world as well as the next, He is the God of the material as well as the spiritual. For me the starting point in our thinking on wealth comes from Jesus' lips:

> *So do not worry, saying, 'What shall we eat?' or 'What shall we drink?' or 'What shall we wear? 'For the pagans run after all these things, and your heavenly Father knows that you need them.* **But seek first his kingdom and his righteousness, and all these things will be given to you as well**. Matthew 6:31–33

Always put the Kingdom and its King first. There are tensions around wealth in both the Old and New Testaments because it has the power to replace God in our lives. There are many warnings about idolatry and about greed; we know that wealth can become an obstacle. The love of money is the root of all evil. So we need to keep choosing God over mammon. Always the Kingdom first. Always the King in His rightful place. But...our Father knows that we need food and drink and clothes and shelter. Money is there to be used for these things. And it is within our capabilities to provide these for ourselves and for our neighbours. If it is within our capabilities then it is our responsibility. As the Pope said, wealth creation is an inescapable duty.

Where does the Pope get these revolutionary ideas? Well, maybe from the Bible. As a 'Living and active' word, the Bible never ceases to challenge and surprise us. We'll come to some shocking stories that Jesus told a little later, but first of all what about the Old Testament? In Deuteronomy God is described as the one 'who gives you the ability to produce wealth'. (Deuteronomy 8:18) With the dreams about seven fat years followed by seven lean years, God gave Joseph a business strategy to save the world from mass starvation. With another dream, and a plan involving spotted and striped sheep, God gave Jacob a way of taking back significant wealth that he was owed by his father in law Laban.

Under their covenant with God, the people of Israel expected God to provide for their material needs. But it is clear in the Old Testament that wealth in itself is not a sign of godliness; the wicked can prosper too. The godly and the ungodly are distinguished from each other not by how much wealth they have, but by how they gain and handle it, or handle the lack of it.

The wife of noble character in Proverbs 31 is held up as a shining example of diligence, acumen, wealth creation and charity. She is a business woman, who understands commerce and investment. 'She considers a field and buys it; out of her earnings she plants a vineyard. She sets about her work vigorously; her arms are strong for her tasks. She sees that her trading is profitable...She makes linen garments and sells them, and supplies the merchants with sashes.'

She is to be praised! But not just because of her ability to create wealth; it is the way she uses wealth that shows she 'fears the Lord'. She provides well for her servants and 'opens her arms to the poor'. As her husband affirms, 'Many women have done excellently, but you surpass them all.' She is indeed worth far more than rubies! Some commentators have even suggested that this wife is a pattern for the Church, the Bride of Christ. The whole passage is quoted at the end of this book.

Some Strange Stories

The stories in the New Testament have a similar spin. The rich young man met with Jesus, wanted eternal life but went away sadly disappointed rather than give away his worldly wealth. This prompted Jesus to make the deliciously visual comment about a camel going through the eye of a needle! And then there's the rich man with the beggar Lazarus sitting at his gate. Despite his wealth, he didn't make it to Abraham's bosom because of his meanness during his life. Yes it's hard for the rich not to get too attached to their money, but, as Jesus says, with God anything is possible.

And Jesus told stories that illustrate something about how we should handle money. Perhaps the best known of these is the one which used to be called the parable of the talents (found in Matthew 25 and Luke 19). But of course, a talent is a weight of silver or gold. The latest translations helpfully call it the parable of the bags of gold. This is a story about money; like many parables it works on other levels too, but money is the theme. It's a Kingdom parable, and its context tells us it's about Jesus, the King, coming back. The slaves were given money, each according to his ability, and expected to use it wisely for the master and account for it when he came back. In the Luke version, the master explains, 'Put this money to work, until I come back.' We'll be judged on how we use the money He's given us. Everything we have is His, and He expects us to use it well...at least to generate interest. Even bankers get a positive mention here! Money works, and the story implies that we should make it work well. The slaves who were commended by the master had doubled what they were given. And then gave it back. The money we have is never ours; in the Kingdom money isn't about possessions, it's about resources.

If that story shocks you, then don't even look at the one in Luke 16! The parable of the unjust steward is a hard one; so hard it's one we rarely preach on. So, let me remind you of the story; here it is, straight from the Bible:

> There was a rich man whose manager was accused of wasting his possessions. So he called him in and asked him, 'What is this I hear about you? Give an account of your management, because you cannot be manager any longer.' The manager said to himself, 'What shall I do now? My master is taking away my job. I'm not strong enough to dig, and I'm ashamed to beg – I know what I'll do so that, when I lose my job here, people will welcome me into their houses.' So he called in each one of his master's debtors. He asked the first, 'How much do you owe my master?' 'Nine hundred gallons of olive oil,' he replied. The manager told him, 'Take your bill, sit down quickly, and make it four hundred and fifty.' Then he asked the second, 'And how much do you owe?' 'A thousand bushels of wheat,' he replied. He told him, 'Take your bill and make it eight hundred.' The master commended the dishonest manager because he had acted shrewdly. For the people of this world are more shrewd in dealing with their own kind than are the people of the light. I tell you, use worldly wealth to gain friends for yourselves, so

*that when it is gone, you will be welcomed into eternal
dwellings.*

Shocking! We could debate for ages the possible meanings
of the passage, we could look at the verses surrounding it,
especially the ones about serving God or Mammon but not
both. But none the less, at the centre of this story is a call to
shrewdness, to be able to use the systems of the world for the
Kingdom. I take it in the same way as Jesus' call to be as
shrewd as snakes. He doesn't want us to be literally like
snakes, and he doesn't want us to be dishonest, like the man in
the story. But He does want us to be shrewd. We can't afford
to be outfoxed by those who know how to use the systems of
the world for their own ends.

John Wesley preached on this passage in his now famous
sermon on money. He summarised his views as 'Having, First,
gained all you can, and, Secondly saved all you can, Then give
all you can'. And I think that's pretty good advice!

And We Conclude?

*From everyone who has been given much, much will be
demanded; and from the one who has been entrusted with
much, much more will be asked.* Luke 12:48

God cares about wealth creation; He has given us abundance,
and it is our work that can help to make that into provision for
all people. If we have the ability to create wealth then we
should do so, in order that it can be distributed. Our wealth,
our money and all our possessions, belong to the King. We
hold them in trust, and it is our duty to use them to help build
His Kingdom.

St Paul is quoted in Acts 20 as saying:

> *You yourselves know that these hands of mine have supplied my own needs and the needs of my companions. In everything I did, I showed you that by this kind of hard work we must help the weak, remembering the words the Lord Jesus himself said: 'It is more blessed to give than to receive.'*

The last chapter was about shaping the world for good and for God. We've discovered in this chapter how wealth creation can change the world for good and help establish Kingdom values. But there is another aspect of building the Kingdom that needs to be considered. Changing it for God involves a spiritual as well as a material change. In the next chapter we will consider what marks out a godly business, a Kingdom building business, a missional business, from something that is simply a good business.

Is this just about tithing or do it apply more widely to the wise use of what we have been given?

What is a Kingdom Building Business?

Our friend Mats Tunehag works for the Lausanne Movement as a senior associate for Business as Mission (BAM), which is another name for Kingdom building business (KBB). Mats has written extensively on BAM, having worked globally with the pioneers of this new mission strategy. And this chapter starts with his excellent definition of BAM, the definition of a business that builds the Kingdom. 'Business as Mission is about real, viable, sustainable and profitable businesses; with a Kingdom of God purpose, perspective and impact; leading to transformation of people and societies spiritually, economically, socially and environmentally – to the greater glory of God.' We're going to look at this definition, give some ideas on how to start a business that fits the definition and then give some examples to see how it works in real life.

A quick word on terminology here; we use BAM and KBB interchangeably in this book and in our material. Other people use the phrase 'transformational business', but this does not necessarily imply a Kingdom agenda. Many things can transform. Other people still use the term Kingdom Business, and this is useful in implying a set of ethics within a business. But is a Kingdom business always missional? BAM and KBB both imply that the businesses are missional, and as such work for the building of the Kingdom of God.

What exactly does this mean

CSR+

In his definition of BAM, Mats refers to changes which are spiritual, economic, social and environmental. These four areas together make up what is called the quadruple bottom line. Some years ago if someone had asked a business 'what's the bottom line', the answer they expected would have been about money. But even secular businesses have moved beyond that and most now use triple bottom line acounting. It's not all about money. So before looking at quadruple, let's look at the triple bottom line.

These days most large corporations have a 'corporate social responsibility', CSR, department. Accountancy and consultancy transnational corporation KPMG describes CSR as 'one of the fastest growing global issues facing all businesses'. It covers the way that businesses 'align their values and behaviour' with the expectations of stakeholders. Stakeholders include customers, investors, employees, suppliers, local communities, regulators, special interest groups and society as a whole. CSR describes a company's apparent commitment to be accountable to these groups in all areas of operation. This includes environmental management, employee and community relations, and also some notion of social justice and human rights. We might decide that these concepts are used somewhat cynically by big companies, but none the less its emergence has led to the widespread use of 'triple bottom line' accounting, where economic, environmental and social performances are all evaluated. Check out the annual report of most businesses these days and you will find discussions on the three bottom lines. *LOOK @ TATA & WIPRO ??*

Mats has also introduced the idea of CSR+. KBB businesspeople need to consider that '+', the spiritual impact of the business. As Mats explains, it's:

...a 4th bottom-line, intentionally revealing and honouring Christ and seeing Him transform lives through business...The + can also be seen as a cross – putting everything under the Lordship of Christ.
(http://www.matstunehag.com/wp-content/uploads/2011/04/The-Mission-of-Business-CSR+1.pdf)

Another way to think of it is as a spiritual footprint. We have all become very used to thinking about the carbon footprint of a business. A spiritual footprint describes how a business affects the spiritual balance where it operates, and beyond.

So, quadruple bottom line, CSR+ or spiritual footprint all describe the way that KBBs need to operate. They need to:

- aim for sustainable financial profitability.
- have a positive social impact.
- have a positive environmental impact.
- have a positive spiritual impact.

Our Quaker forebears used as their motto 'spiritual and solvent'. That is good guidance for us too! Unless our businesses are profitable they will not stay in business. One business that we spent some time with was a creative play group for under 5s. The business had a wonderful spiritual impact; the two founders walked alongside the parents, befriended and pastored them in a natural and genuine way, and gave them hope and purpose through the good news. But the business is struggling to make enough money to cover the costs, and might have to close down. All that potential spiritual impact for the future could be lost.

And so we must always have an eye on the financial bottom line. But the other bottom lines help to make a business worthwhile, because they show what impact the money and the business are having. For example, creating local employment has a positive social impact. Employing people who are otherwise at risk, for example from the sex trade, has an even greater social impact. Some Fairtrade businesses can demonstrate an environmental impact as well as a social one, where trade justice is an aim of the business. Consideration of pollution and carbon footprint are important too. This much other businesses do too, and Kingdom business cannot be less than equal with secular businesses when it comes to the triple bottom line. Remember those quotes from Richard Branson in chapter 1? The world out there is really grasping the idea of using businesses to shape the world for good. But what about shaping it for God? That is where our triple bottom line becomes a quadruple bottom line. We must take into account the spiritual impact.

KBBs have a spiritual impact, and that is both integrated into the other three bottom lines and overarches all of them. The one thing it isn't is divorced from them. That would be a sacred secular divide! How we handle our money is part of our spiritual impact. How we relate to the communities inside and outside of the business is part of our spiritual impact. How we treat creation, the environment, is part of our spiritual impact.

But what is a Spiritual Bottom Line?

The spiritual bottom line is our unique flavour, so what exactly is it and how do we measure it? Spiritual impact can be on employees, on clients or customers, or on a surrounding community. Of course all KBBs are expected to demonstrate Christian values and business ethics, about which more below; this is a minimum requirement. And this can be a genuine part of a spiritual bottom line, because it witnesses to Kingdom values, and integrity can call out integrity in the other, changing the temperature of a contact network. And in my experience people actually like having integrity called out of them; it creates a positive (spiritual?) feeling. But beyond that, a spiritual bottom line must speak to people of meaning and purpose, which people are hungry for. In his book *The Hungry Spirit*, Charles Handy wrote:

> *In Africa they say there are two hungers, the lesser hunger and the greater hunger. The lesser hunger is for the things that sustain life...The greater hunger is for an answer to the question 'why?' for some understanding of what life is for.*

Whereas the social and environmental bottom lines are about good news, and that is important, it is the spiritual bottom line that speaks of good news for eternity, and not just for this time.

One thing that distinguishes the post modern era from the modern is the widespread acceptance of a need for spirituality. The world now talks about things spiritual, and so Christians are allowed to too! Talking about a spiritual bottom line is not considered very strange at a time when even big secular corporations are hiring spiritual consultants to help motivate their workforce.

But what do people mean by the word spirituality? It is perhaps one of the most post modern of words, a Humpty-Dumpty word, which means entirely what the user wants it to mean. Definitions I have found used by non-Christians include:

Spirituality is not religion; it is not about beliefs, creeds or dogmas. It is about being fully alive, relationships and that which gives meaning and purpose.

Spirituality combines our basic philosophy towards life, our vision and our values, with our conduct and our practices. Spirituality encompasses our ability to tap into our deepest

41

resources, that part of ourselves which is unseen and mysterious to develop our fullest potential.

Spirituality is a basic feeling of being connected with one's complete self, others and the entire universe. If a single word best captures the meaning of spirituality and the vital role it plays in people's lives, that word is 'interconnectedness'.

Spirituality is a quest for the sacred, involving a person's identity, values and worldview.

Spirituality points to our interiors, our subjective life, as contrasted to the objective domain of material events and objects.

There is ambivalence and lack of agreement in these definitions. However, many people agree that, whatever it is, spirituality reaches their areas of need. And in their understanding of it we can find ways to talk about Christian spirituality.

And so, back to the spiritual bottom line. In the story told at the beginning of the Bible, the story of Adam and Eve and the separation that came between them and God, there's a description of the way people still feel today. They feel cut off from each other, from creation, from their work and from their full potential; this all comes because they are cut off from God, the One who gives it all meaning and purpose. It is this alienation that people still want to be healed from, and that is what comes from their heart in the cry for spirituality. They want real relationships, connectedness with the universe, a fulfilling of their own potential, a tapping into something unseen and mysterious and a quest for the sacred. We can use this language, their language, in expressing what we mean by our spiritual bottom line. It is about making people 'fully alive', it's about giving them meaning and purpose because they are reconnected with 'the sacred'.

A positive social impact might well help to fill the lesser hunger, but the greater hunger will still be there. A positive environmental impact will help stewardship of the planet, but will not help people to reconnect with creation. God is not indifferent to these things; when the Kingdom comes in its fullness there will be justice and an end to exploitation of people and the rest of creation. But there will be more than that. Because the King will be here we will be fully the people that we were created to be, knowing our value and purpose, and having a relationship with Him that satisfies all our hungers. Our spiritual bottom line in businesses today is putting Christ at the centre and helping His Kingdom break through in the area where we operate, so that the people we influence and affect can feel those Kingdom benefits here and now.

How can we measure a spiritual bottom line? That's harder! How does a church measure its spiritual impact? We can tell how many people come through the door, but not how much the Kingdom is growing in them and through them. And from the stories that Jesus told, the Kingdom is not just about numbers. There is rejoicing over the one. There might be encounters we're involved in which have been very significant for the other people involved but where we don't get to hear the outcome. So perhaps it's counter-Kingdom to even try to measure spiritual impact. We must aim to have a spiritual bottom line, but it is the Lord who measures it. It seems to me that the important thing is to keep throwing out those mustard seeds, and keep on watering them, regardless of whether or not we see how the Lord grows them!

Business Ethics

That KBBs should operate ethically should go without saying...but I'm going to say it anyway! The Bible has a lot to say about business ethics. Integrity and honesty are called for. In the Law:

> *Do not use dishonest standards when measuring length, weight or quantity. Use honest scales and honest weights, an honest ephah and an honest hin.* Leviticus 19:35, 36

In the prophets:

> *Hear this, you who trample the needy and do away with the poor of the land, saying, 'When will the New Moon be over that we may sell grain, and the Sabbath be ended that we may market wheat?'– skimping on the measure, boosting the price and cheating with dishonest scales, buying the poor with silver and the needy for a pair of sandals, selling even the sweepings with the wheat. The Lord has sworn by himself, the Pride of Jacob: 'I will never forget anything they have done'.* Amos 8:4–7

Both the Old and New Testament talk about treating those who work for you well. Colossians 4 asks masters to treat workers fairly, because we know that we also have a master in heaven. James writes:

> *Look! The wages you failed to pay the workmen who mowed your fields are crying out against you. The cries of the harvesters have reached the ears of the Lord Almighty.* James 5:4

And Paul sums it up pretty well in his letter to the church in Rome:

> *Give to everyone what you owe them: If you owe taxes, pay taxes; if revenue, then revenue; if respect, then respect; if honour, then honour. Let no debt remain outstanding, except the continuing debt to love one another, for whoever loves others has fulfilled the law. The commandments...are*

summed up in this one command: 'Love your neighbour as yourself'. Romans 13:7–9

Tax evasion, underpaying workers, providing poor quality products, charging customers more than necessary are all unloving actions. In the end, integrity and honesty are ways to demonstrate love. And to demonstrate Kingdom values to your network of contacts, from employees, to suppliers to the bank manager.

Read Proverbs 31 again and see the honourable way to do business!

And We Conclude?

No one can serve two masters. For you will hate one and love the other; you will be devoted to one and despise the other. You cannot serve both God and mammon. Matthew 6:24

If we're working in business can we remain spiritually neutral? Is there a middle ground where we can operate that doesn't require us to be thinking with our Christian heads on, but where we can just fit in with the prevailing climate we're working in?

To remain spiritually neutral implies that there is a spiritual neutrality to be had! I'm not sure that the Bible leads us to believe that. At the beginning of the last century the German scholar Max Weber wrote that capitalism represented 'the disenchantment of the world'. Many people would question that conclusion these days. It seems more likely in hindsight that capitalism is itself a sort of enchantment. In the 19th century Thomas Carlyle had written that capitalism 'bears the gospel of Mammonism' and renders its devotees 'spell bound'.

It seems that capitalism is not just another spirituality, it is one that is evangelistic, spreading itself across the whole world, changing lifestyles...turning people into consumers. And when we see the effects of consumerism on the lives of those affected by it, spell bound does seem a reasonable way to look at it. People are driven into debt and beyond through being held in its sway.

Jesus warned that we can't serve both God and mammon. Mammon has been translated variously as money or wealth, but neither really captures the idea of mammon that I think Jesus is talking about. It's more personal than that. He says mammon can be a master in the same way that God is; it can suck the true life out of us and leave us worrying about what to eat, or drink or wear instead of developing a trusting relationship with God. It is a false god; and we can develop an alternative spirituality based on serving that god.

Can we remain spiritually neutral? I don't think so. If we're not serving the Spirit of God, then we might find that we're serving the Spirit of Capitalism. And for our businesses that means that whether we intend it or not there IS a spiritual bottom line. We do have a spiritual footprint. We need to make sure that it glorifies God.

Some Examples

We've talked about how KBBs are set up and about their spiritual impact. So how does this work out in reality? There are many Kingdom building businesses around the world, and we've picked out just a few examples that we know. Here are some businesses that are putting theory into practice.

CSR+ in action

There is one case study that we feel passionate about; we want to include it so you can feel passionate about it too! But in order to do that, because of security issues, we have to withhold some of the details. None the less, the story is real and it is inspiring.

A missionary family felt called to move to a new continent, to a specific town. They had no idea what lay ahead, but they knew they had a mission with Jesus to the poor and oppressed in that place. As they explain, The Message version of a verse in John's Gospel spoke to them, 'The Word became flesh and blood, and moved into the neighbourhood'. And after moving into their flat it took very little time to discover who their neighbours were; women trapped in prostitution. Not originally thinking of a business programme, the couple started to think and pray around the question 'how does the Kingdom of God manifest itself in a neighbourhood like this?'.

They came to realise that prostitution is an economic problem, a form of exploitation of the poor; most women working as prostitutes don't choose the work they do, it chooses them. And they have no alternative. Girls and young women are trafficked across the world for the sex industry. In some cases they are sold by their parents (who have nothing else to sell and many hungry mouths to feed), in some cases stolen and in some cases tricked into thinking they are being taken to a city to do a respectable job. It's big business; virgins command a high price when they are sold on to those running the sex industry. Apart from trafficked women there are those who have hit rock bottom, maybe widowed with young children, and nothing else to sell except their bodies. For all these women, what is the good news that the Kingdom has to offer?

The Kingdom solution to an economic problem like trafficking and prostitution is also economic. These women needed alternative employment, needed to be given a choice which previously had not existed for them. And so a business was set up to employ them, making items that would be sold across the world. This is a real business, which has now been in business for over a decade. It employs many women, and has moved them from slavery to freedom. They have the freedom to enjoy dignified employment, in an enduring community of healing, faith and hope. It's real Kingdom work!

And the women know that it is Jesus who has set them free. The original founder, who moved into the neighbourhood, still runs the business and says:

> *Time and time again the women seem to understand more of who Jesus is than I do. Throughout the Gospels it's the little people, the poor, the unlovely and unloved that seem to have a greater understanding of who Jesus is and what He's about. If we are seeking to be a Kingdom business we need this kind of insight and input. It's too easy to think that we need to leave the running of the business to those who are educated and have a business mind.*

The women now take the lead in shaping and running the business. He also recalls a time he took one of his employees to a local area where prostitutes were working. She had been trafficked at the age of 13, and, although illiterate, she is now a visionary and leader in the business. She suggested that they expand into this new area, and go to talk to the women there about the alternative they could offer. He explains:

I thought she would start by talking about the business and the new jobs they could have. But at the very beginning of the discussion, after listening to what they wanted she said 'So you want real freedom do you? You need to start praying to Jesus. He's the one who gives real freedom.'

It's hard work. But it transforms lives and communities. This is Kingdom building at work, and our heartfelt desire is that there should be more of it. Imagine how the world could be changed if businesses like this sprang up all around the world!

Building the Kingdom through...Building!

Jon Barber was working for a Japanese multi-national electronics company as their Global Pricing Manager focusing on Eastern European and Asian markets. A long term Christian, he recognised that two dreams that he had were significant. In the first he was woken at 3am with a vision of tradesmen in his home, singing worship songs with tears rolling down their cheeks. In the second he had a picture of a bowl of spaghetti bolognaise; the Lord was telling him to form a building company where Christians and non-Christians would work together with the Christians like bolognaise sauce coating and impacting non-Christians like spaghetti. The two were to be mixed and God would do the rest! Jon explains, 'Jesus said just follow me, and they will follow you and the other Christians on site. Just bring them into the business and I will invade their lives.'

And so Rock Solid Building was born. But there was another surprise; just as Jon was about to register the limited company, his employer offered him redundancy, with six months gardening leave as notice of redundancy. It was perfect God timing and further confirmation from God to leap into a new career.

For the first 15 months Jon teamed up with a non-believer who had 25 years experience and excellent building skills. Jon supported him as a hands on apprentice while bringing strong customer service and business management skills that he had acquired from his previous careers. The partnership worked well and Jon quickly got to grips with his new vocation.

The non-believer became Jon's foreman and Rock Solid progressed to the point where it could take on two substantial commercial contracts involving the conversion of derelict office premises into high-quality modern offices and a luxury leisure facility. These commercial projects lasted 15 months and at one point involved 16 subcontractors on site with a mixture of Christian and non-Christians – the dream had become a reality and God turned up.

On site the Holy Spirit began His work of pointing non-believers to Jesus. Most opened up easily to their Christian counterparts, giving numerous opportunities for discussion, debate and prayer. The non-Christians were changing before Jon's eyes. They were becoming disciples as they followed the Christians, attracted by the practical support Jesus gave them in their daily lives. 'There must be something in this Christianity' became a common phrase! Jon says:

The impact varied from informal conversations about Jesus to one guy receiving some intimate Christian counselling for alcohol and drug related issues. Men were being touched by God on a building site who would only ever enter a church for a wedding or a funeral. What took me completely by surprise was the way that the spirit of Jesus directly hit some of these tough working class men head on. On three occasions men broke down in tears under conviction of the Holy Spirit.

He talks about it as 'weeping in repentance', as men confessed how dirty they felt and how empty their lives were, with one man even falling on his knees in the dust and dirt of a building site and sobbing. Jon found he had to go back into Church history to discover similar events at the meetings of John Wesley and Moody and most markedly by General Booth, founder of the Salvation Army. Jon admits that William Booth is more of a role model for him than most people in the modern Church, because the events seen in Booth's ministry have happened in Rock Solid.

I originally thought the message to non-Christian tradesmen was 'build and believe in Jesus'. Now I say 'build, repent and be baptised.' These men want to hear the truth of the gospel and I so want Rock Solid to be a vehicle for that while also being a building company of excellence. The journey continues.

Reshaping Financial Products

Gavin has worked in the financial services business for 25 years. A moment of revelation came when he was watching a scene from the film *Titanic* of all films! The 'unsinkable' ship had hit an iceberg and the first class passengers, who had access to the lifeboats, were wearing life jackets, drinking champagne and listening to the music being played for them by the orchestra. Meanwhile the passengers in steerage were screaming, locked below deck as the ship sank:

> *This resonated with me as a picture of our world. I saw myself as one of the first class passengers in life (in the context of the picture, living in the relative comfort of healthy family and community relationships as well as a developed country), and as we raise the volume of the music of the busy world around us this blocks out the screams of those who are trapped in poverty whether it be material or relational in our society or the developing world.*

We live in a culture of choices, and yet we don't always use the choice that is available. There are choices about investing our money, but even as Christian investors we don't always choose to have our money making the impact in the world that it could. We might invest our money in any sort of pot (and a pension plan is just that sort of pot) and then use the money we've made to give to 'good causes'. But we don't know how that money has been made; it might have been invested in a business that works against the good causes we want to support. Gavin saw a vision which encouraged investment to flow to places where people have a need for capital; money to fund businesses which meet the social needs of vulnerable people and communities. 'It's about trying to build a model of justice and intentional social responsibility into the financial marketplace.'

In 2009 he launched his own business, to carry through the vision. The company is a financial services business established to distribute 'impact investment' products to the retail market through Independent Financial Advisers. Impact investments are investments which are **intentionally** using capital to generate positive social and/or environmental impact beyond a financial profit, a model based on the quadruple bottom line. It specifically targets transformation of individuals, communities and society as a whole. This innovative way of investing appeals to people outside the Church too. There is a turning of the tide and a momentum gathering in the financial services world around this approach to investment. It is starting to be recognised as having the potential to be a driving force for change, enabling the Financial Services Industry to reclaim its place in society as a means of supporting and empowering social and economic progress in the world.

Blessing the Community with Cheesecake: a Case Study by Mats Tunehag

Our friend and colleague Mats Tunehag travelled to Istanbul and wrote this case study, which he has kindly allowed us to use.

Maria Perdue is an American who loves to bake. But she never imagined she would become a successful businesswoman in Istanbul. Now she makes cheesecakes based on her mum's recipe and customers travel for hours to visit her shop.

Istanbul is a huge, sprawling city with a lot of charm. It has a fascinating history (even the Vikings went there!) and it is beautifully situated at the Bosporus. I took the ferry across the continents, from Europe to Asia, and from there a noisy bus to the very outskirts of the 12 million people strong city. An hour and a half later we arrived in the village where Maria lives and works.

Technically Turkey is a secular state and many parts of Istanbul certainly have a Western European feel, albeit with an oriental touch. But the Islamic influence is nevertheless real and tangible. The village where Maria has her café is relatively

Muslim and conservative. 'In the beginning some were suspicious, wondering who we were and what we were up to. Some even tried to chase us and our customers away', says Maria. A neighbouring shop even had a sign up warning people to not buy any cheesecakes 'from the evil missionary'.

But Maria kept running the café. Her kindness, integrity, professionalism and – of course – her tasty products made her gradually accepted and now she is respected part of the community. Sure, Maria is a follower of Jesus – she has never tried to hide that fact. But she is a businesswoman with a passion to serve her customers and suppliers, her staff and the community where she lives.

She has three women employees, all dressed conservatively and covered. Maria is considering hiring a fourth woman. Her business is thriving. 'I speak openly and frankly with my staff, telling them I have two hats: on the one hand I am a friend and colleague. But I also need to put on the other hat at times; the businesswoman and CEO. You need both to be able to both care for staff but also succeed as a business', says Maria. 'And if the company doesn't prosper it will be detrimental also for my employees.'

The small and cosy café has an interior design which is quite exquisite. It is also very clean! Her business has three main revenue sources: the biggest is take-away; the second is other bakeries selling her products and thirdly people eating in the café.

Turkish media has recognised her products and café. Just before my visit a Turkish TV-team had been there. The large Turkish daily *Hürriyet* wrote: 'With her cheesecakes Maria uses all natural products, no additives, leaving you as light in the head as the creation itself. The cherries and strawberries from their own garden make each bite sublime and the sauces are the stuff of Black Sea lore'.

Maria's Cheesecakes is a respected brand name which gradually is becoming more known. The bulk of her customers

travel from afar to buy her delicious cakes. The influx of
people also benefits other businesses in the village.

Do you draw people into the neighborhood? What do they do while they are there?

And We Conclude?

The businesses we have highlighted here are examples of
many across the world. These have been set up by individuals,
but we are increasingly aware of churches setting up
businesses to help impact their local communities. We have
heard of a milkshake bar set up by a church to provide
training and employment to some local youngsters, and a fun
place to hang out for others who are customers. And Shaun
Lambert has written about his church's coffee house in his
book, *A Book of Sparks*. And the leaders from yet another
church have set up an estate agency on the high street. The
vision is spreading!

These are real, viable, sustainable and profitable businesses
with a Kingdom impact, and transformation is happening. If
you want to join in with this, then read on!

How Can I Set Up a Kingdom Business?

I Have a Business Idea...What do I do?

One of us recently did a short slot on a mainstream UK TV channel talking about business and God. Just a couple of minutes, but I managed to get some of the key points across (http://www.4thought.tv/themes/is-it-right-to-ask-god-to-make-us-rich/rev-bridget-adams?autoplay=true). Many of the secular audience were (of course!) sceptical. One comment posted afterwards read:

> There's no easy way to make a business successful. The usual method is to work extremely hard, though some people appear to make money by sheer brilliance. What would God do to make a business work?

It's a fair enough question. And yet it is the experience of many of us that He does! Hard work is still required. But maybe sheer brilliance isn't, because that's one of the things that God supplies! In fact He specialises in it. So perhaps the first thing to note about starting a KBB is that God takes the lead and we follow. Business ideas can come inspirationally in an instant, almost like a download, or more slowly, with an inkling here and a feeling there. Either way, there's a lot of prayer involved. If you look at our case studies in the next chapter you will see what we mean. A dream, a revelation, a word...God can lead us in many ways when we let Him. So here are some steps that lead us through the process of setting up a KBB.

Begin with God

He is the Lord. He is the CEO. As Christians we are called to partner God in His plans for this world. This may or may not be in business. What is God calling you to do? And if it is business, what type of business is God calling you to set up? And where? In this town, in this country, or somewhere abroad? This time is about prayer and discernment. Involve someone else if you can, a friend or colleague, or better still a potential business partner. Read the section below about teams and their biblical basis and effectiveness. We are rarely called to do something completely on our own; we work as a body. God might be calling a small group or a whole church into this business idea. So pray about who is in your team. If you are married, then it should go without saying that your spouse is in your team and needs to be deeply involved in this phase. In this discerning time you might find that your church will offer some support. Also, some organisations offer help in this area; see our directory at the end of this book.

Put the Business Idea Down on Paper

If the business idea takes hold of you and your team, then the next stage is putting it down on paper. Writing and listening, then writing more and listening again; this process needs to be done in partnership with God, seeking His direction.

Go Deeper

Having got the initial thoughts down, it is now time to go deeper. Here a business plan will prove to be very useful. You can get these from good online websites about starting a business. Alternatively there are various books out there. A common mistake by new businesses is inadequate market research and weak financial planning. Spending time doing a detailed business plan will help you to not only shape your business idea but test it to see if it is a viable option. Once again this process should involve a continuing conversation with God.

So what does a typical business plan look like? They differ greatly, but some of the key areas would include: a summary of the business; it's vision and goals; what is unique about this business and where its niche will be; where the business will operate from and what geographical areas will it cover; market research to ascertain if the product/service is sellable and that there is demand for it; profiling competitors; analysing start up costs and ongoing costs for running the business; how much money will be required to promote/advertise the business; a profit and loss forecast and a cash flow forecast. All this may sound like a lot of work but if you are truly serious about setting up a business this is a good time investment. Many a business has failed due to lack of planning and research. Once the business plan is done, it is worthwhile getting assistance in looking over it to test it, help with modifications and ascertain whether further research is required.

Does this Work?

At the end of your going deeper phase you should have some confidence that there is a market for whatever product or service you are selling, that your business will make enough profit to cover the costs and that it will have a positive social, environmental and spiritual impact. You will also know how much money you need to start you off. Even a business that will make a profit needs money at the beginning as the costs come before the sales...unfortunately! And before you make any money from the business, you will still need money to live on. So be realistic about how much you need, and how you can get financial input. Some people we've talked to have enough in their savings or in a redundancy package (for example) to finance their business. Some find investors; but choosing investors for a KBB also needs a lot of prayer. You need backers who are in tune with your quadruple bottom

RIF

line. Avoiding misunderstandings at the beginning will save you a lot of trouble later.

You will probably need suppliers too, other businesses that will supply or make to order things that you need for your product or service. So now is the time to start finding these; again prayer and recommendations are invaluable. Your business can be pulled down by suppliers whose quality or reliability is poor. Your reputation will be tarnished by theirs. More research required!

So, now you've got your vision, have developed your plan and have your finance in place. It's time to get started.

Get Started

There are financial and legal requirements to setting up a business. These will be different in different countries. Wherever you are, there will be various websites that can offer you advice and tools for starting up. However, more detailed advice can be gained from accountants. A good accountant is an enormous help to a new business and it is worth spending some time finding one, preferably through personal recommendation from another Christian business person. The accountant doesn't have to be a Christian, but he or she needs to have the right level of integrity to understand the level of righteousness you want to see in your business.

An accountant can help with setting things up such as registering a company, which needn't be expensive. They can also advise on how to keep accounts and filing systems throughout the year as this will assist you when you come to do your annual tax accounts. Some other areas to consider when getting started will include setting up a bank account and registering business email addresses.

BAM in a Box

Setting up a business is not easy, but you can find plenty of help along the way. We've already mentioned God (who provides invaluable help!) and other Christian business people and groups. There is a directory at the end of this book of really useful organisations.

Maybe you feel called to set up a business but you're not a natural high-level entrepreneur. As Mats Tunehag writes:

> *There are just a few Bill Gates, Microsoft, and Ingvar Kamprad, IKEA, who can start from scratch and build big. There are a few others who can start from an idea and develop a growing business small to medium size. But how are we to tap into the many medium-level entrepreneurial people who also are good managers, but won't start from nothing, as it were? People in this category can often run a franchise successfully, a McDonalds, a Starbucks, a Chick-fil-A, etc... These are businesses in a box: unpack, read the manual and go.*

The idea of franchisable KBBs is being developed through a global initiative called BAM in a Box; the idea is to develop a set of ready to run businesses that can help to build the Kingdom. A franchise will make entry to market much easier, wherever you are in the world. Through taking a franchise rather than building your own business from scratch, you will still be using your local knowledge and networks, but will have many other things taken care of by the franchiser; for example suppliers, high level marketing and method of operation. To find out more, watch the process unfold through the BAM Think Tank (bamthinktank.org).

And to find out more read Mats' article on BAM in a Box on www.matstunehag.com/wp-content/uploads/2011/04/BAM-in-a-Box-article.pdf.

Teams Work!

> *Do not conform to the pattern of this world, but be transformed by the renewing of your mind. Then you will be able to test and approve what God's will is — his good, pleasing and perfect will. For by the grace given me I say to every one of you: Do not think of yourself more highly than you ought, but rather think of yourself with sober judgment, in accordance with the faith God has distributed to each of you. For just as each of us has one body with many members, and these members do not all have the same function, so in Christ we, though many, form one body, and each member belongs to all the others. We have different gifts, according to the grace given to each of us.* Romans 12:2–6

We don't have to be conditioned by the way that the world runs businesses. In fact, all the good ideas were in the Bible in the first place! Some are so good that they have been taken up by the rest of the world. And team building is one of them; working together as a body, using our different skills and gifts. But as Christians we don't have to stop there. As St Paul would say, we can show them the most excellent way. Love. Read 1 Corinthians 13 again with businesses in mind. This is how teams really work; *'Love is patient, love is kind. It does not envy, it does not boast, it is not proud. It does not dishonour others, it is not self-seeking, it is not easily angered, it keeps no record of wrongs. Love does not delight in evil but rejoices with the truth. It always protects, always trusts, always hopes, always perseveres.'* Is your business ready for that? Or, come to think of it, is mine? But when we are, wow what team work will follow!

There are many books and tools available to help analyse your personality type and how you would work best in a team. One useful one is StrengthsFinder, produced by the Gallup organisation (www.strengthsfinder.com). But here is a summary of just one model for a leadership team which I have found extremely useful. It has several advantages. It is insightful; it is simple to explain and understand; it was developed at Warwick Business School by Nigel Sykes, Principal Teaching Fellow in the Entrepreneureship and Innovation Group; it is useful in entrepreneurial organisations and it has a biblical basis.

The model outlines the 3 Es and their 3 Ps. Let me explain. The first E is the envisioner. And the P that goes with this E is possibilities. The envisioner understands possibilities, and principles. The envisioner sees big ideas. It is as if s/he is sitting in the crow's nest, or riding on the back of an eagle. Everything is there to be seen. S/he has a tendency to expansive thinking which breaks the mould, and can therefore sometimes be seen as creative destruction. As children envisioners take things apart to see how they work! The envisioner has great ideas, maybe too many of them, and has less interest in seeing them come to fruition than in identifying them. Although s/he can cope with sufficient detail to see where the idea sits, the envisioner is not generally good at detail. But gifted and creative envisioners are the source of all good ideas.

The next E is the enabler, and s/he understands processes. The enabler provides a safe pair of hands. S/he is a good organiser and motivator, good with systems and good with people. S/he can interpret the vision and from that will gather and release information to help and support it. The enabler has a natural talent to harmonise, to manage and to set up systems that allow the envisioner's vision to become reality.

The final E is the enactor, who understands practicalities. The enactor is a focused 'do-er'. S/he sticks to the task and sees it through to completion. The enactor keeps the team on its toes; like a thumb for the fingers, s/he provides a balancing force for the other functions. Like a point man in the army, the enactor goes ahead, moves out, marking out the territory and then waiting for the rest of the team to catch up, so that s/he can move out again. In order to be so focused, the enactor must have a smaller but none the less powerful vision, seeing details rather than the whole terrain.

Together the 3 Es are a Dream Team for leadership; the envisioner, enabler and enactor work together, taking care of the possibilities, the processes and the practicalities to advance the group vision, first grasped by the envisioner and then shared in the team. The vision becomes a precious item around which they will rally. And within the team the leadership baton can be passed round, each one taking the lead as appropriate.

The 3 Es are like different elements; the envisioner is like water, hard to harness but, like a swirling sea, full of energy and refreshment; the enabler is like sand, a safe place for fire and water to meet, providing stability, mouldable and a place to mould; the enactor is like fire, igniting everything else and making a noticeable impact.

With one E missing, leadership teams can be fatally unbalanced. Nigel gives each 2 E combo a title. With no envisioner we have 'analysis and no hope'. There might be a temptation to think that a good idea can be plucked from somewhere and that it is really enablers and enactors who make the enterprise tick. This would result in a team of great harmonisers and finishers, but with no vision. With only enactors and enablers in the team, analysis paralysis can result. This will be an enterprise that misses the main chance and is extremely poor at coping with change in the marketplace or environment.

With no enabler we have 'steam and confusion'. Water and fire make a very volatile mix. By rejecting the enabler, there is no harmoniser, and the team is characterised by conflict, with feelings of rejection and denial. Some enterprises storm their way through this, but it will always be an uncomfortable place to work with at best erratic growth.

No enactor leads to 'ideas and no action'. With only envisioners and enablers in the team there is great enthusiasm and clear direction, but no settlers to complete the work. There can be lots of vision, creativity and great ideas, but no action. An enterprise with just these 2 Es might start well, but it cannot survive in the long term.

Nigel's full model includes a very useful analysis of how businesses grow and develop. Butterflies grow from eggs, and go through stages of development. It is the same for enterprises; they don't just get bigger, they change.

Did you get the Bible part of the model? In the Old Testament there are three kinds of leaders; prophets, priests and kings. It's similar in the New Testament, with prophets, pastors and apostles. The three Es correspond to these biblical leader types; the envisioner is the prophet, the enabler is the priest or pastor, the enactor is the 'king' or apostle. It's good to know that over thousands of years these three leader types have worked together!

So, which E are you? And the rest of your team? Watch out for those fatally unbalanced duos! Although team leadership is ideal, you might be starting on your own. By knowing which E you are, you know who you are looking out for to be in your team. Get that team together as soon as possible, because vision that can hit the ground running comes from a team dreaming together.

Spider or Starfish?

So now you've got the idea and you're going to set up a business, with a team in place, how will you organise your company for success? In their 2006 book *The Starfish and the Spider*, Brafman and Beckstrom suggested that organisations structured like starfish can be more successful than traditional spider shaped ones. The analogy comes from biology;

although starfish and spiders may look similar, in fact they are very different. Spiders have a head, containing a brain; starfish have a distributed neurological function. Cut the head off a spider and it dies; cut the arm off a starfish and you probably end up with two starfish. In organisational terms, spiders are those with a rigid hierarchy and top-down leadership, where the corporate vision resides in the 'head'. Starfish organisations are decentralised and rely on the power of shared vision and peer relationships. They are communities where people are motivated. They are more flexible than their spider-like counterparts, and can therefore react more quickly to changes.

Although the Brafman and Beckstrom book is subtitled 'the unstoppable power of leaderless organisations', starfish concerns are far from leaderless. But they do rely on a different leadership style. Leaders in a spider organisation use a 'command and control' style. Starfish organisations foster 'enable and release' management styles. Brafman and Beckstrom use the Apache tribe as a historical model of a decentralised organisation. The Apache had a Nan'tan, a spiritual and cultural leader. Geronimo is perhaps the best known of these. Nan'tans didn't command; coercion was a foreign concept to the Apaches. But if Geronimo started fighting, then it was very likely that people would join him because experience led them to trust and respect his vision.

In fact, when it comes to leadership, the roles Brafman and Beckstrom identify relate to the 3 E model outlined above. In an entrepreneurial team, Brafman and Beckstrom's spiritual catalyst seems to be what we have called the envisioner. They also identify a 'champion': 'A champion is relentless in promoting a new idea... A catalyst's charisma, like that of the Nan'tans, has a subtlety to it...there's nothing subtle about the champion.' They also note that champions are hyperactive, but are not organisers or connectors. This then is our enactor. What of the enabler? Well, I suspect that they are there in the companies Brafman and Becktrom describe. Crucial to the operation of a decentralised organisation is what they call the 'circle', that is the community in which the distributed vision resides. Although this is not explicit in their description, a community does not come into being or stay in existence without an enabler to organise it.

So it seems that the essential leadership roles even in a starfish company can be categorised into the 3 Es. The flatness of the starfish structure points the way to developing and growing an entrepreneurial company. To build hierarchies will not be the most productive way forward, but to find ways of engaging all employees with the vision will be.

The book identifies a very successful, contemporary starfish organisation: al Qaeda. Does the death of bin Laden mean the death of al Qaeda? Almost certainly not. It's not a spider that dies when its head is cut off! The vision has been distributed and taken up by many people in many countries. Starfish are much more resilient than spiders.

Of course, the Church has known about this for a long time. The growth of the house church movement in China is one example. And that great church planter St Paul knew a thing or two about distributing vision and enabling and releasing new Christians. 'Brothers and sisters, join in imitating me, and observe those who live according to the example you have in us.' (Philippians 3:17) Like Geronimo, Paul expected to be imitated. But beyond that there are lessons for our businesses. Brafman and Beckstrom give examples of companies and ventures like Wikipedia, eBay and Skype, but also General Electric and Toyota, which are examples of hybrid companies, incorporating the best of spiders and starfish. What these companies have in common, apart from the starfish nature of significant parts of their operation, is their business success. In the 21st century there are new rules to the game, and starfish have the upper hand.

The Son is the image of the invisible God, the firstborn over all creation. For in him all things were created: things in heaven and on earth, visible and invisible, whether thrones or powers or rulers or authorities; all things have been created through him and for him. He is before all things, and in him all things hold together. And he is the head of the body, the church; he is the beginning and the firstborn from among the dead, so that in everything he might have the supremacy. For God was pleased to have all his fullness dwell in him, and through him to reconcile to himself all things, whether things on earth or things in heaven, by making peace through his blood, shed on the cross. Colossians 1:15–19

Well, in truth we didn't need the final verse but it is far too good to leave out! We really only needed the discussion about head and body. There is only one 'head', and that is Jesus. The rest is body; that's us. It's interesting that 'head' has more than one meaning, and St Paul seems to use two meanings in this one passage. We sometimes use 'head' to mean source or beginning, as in the head of a river, and that seems to be one of the meanings hinted at here. Jesus is the source of creation. He is before all things. But he is also a head like the head of a body, and has supremacy. He truly IS the CEO!

Leadership Jesus Style!

How can we consider leadership in a Christian context without explicitly mentioning Jesus? Well, He certainly enabled and released the apostles! He built teams and equipped them; the distributed vision that was ignited at Pentecost spread like wildfire. Jesus was the only one of us who was all 3 Es; He was and is prophet, priest and king. But in addition, His explicit example of servant leadership is powerful. How can we be servant leaders too? Leadership should never resort to 'lording' it over others or 'exercising authority' over them (as in Mark 10:41–43). If we aspire to leadership in business, it must be servant leadership. And it must also be inspirational, sharing and building vision as we've outlined above. In Jesus' own ministry storytelling was a key part of doing just that; his parables included told stories (for example the sower and the seed, the lost son or sheep or coin) and acted stories (for example the washing of the disciples feet, turning water into wine, the appointment of 12 Jewish men as disciples). If we're not using command and control, but instead trying to build up shared vision to enable and release, then we too need to learn about storytelling.

The secular world has recently realised this too. 'Storytelling is the single most powerful tool in a leader's toolkit', according to Dr. Howard Gardner, the author of *Changing Minds*, and a Harvard University professor. According to *The Leaders Guide to Storytelling* (Denning, 2005) storytelling can be used to: motivate others to action, build trust – in me, in us – transmit values, get others to work together, share knowledge, tame the grapevine, create and share vision. Stories can be used inside or outside; brand development often relies on storytelling. But I want to concentrate on stories told inside an organisation, storytelling as a management tool rather than a marketing tool.

Each of the leadership types that we've looked at can use storytelling from their strengths. In this I would suggest that it is most natural for the prophet to tell the big story (which distributes vision), the pastor to tell 'our' story (which makes bonds and builds communities) and the apostle to tell, or even act out, 'my' story (which gives a practical example to follow). In the Bible it is the prophets who tell the big story. For example, Hosea was called to live out the story of God and Israel (as explained in Hosea 1:2–11). The Kings or apostles (including Paul) generate stories which inspire and give an example (for example see Philippians 3:4–14). And it is in the gathered people of God context that the pastors/priests tend to lead the people in remembering the story that binds them together. In the OT it is the story of the exodus that binds the people together and is alluded to many times. The Pesach Seder celebrated by Jews each year retells the whole story in a stylised way, as commanded in the OT. In the Christian community we remember our story in the communion service.

Leaders need stories; do you know the big story, our story or even your story as it relates to your company or organisation? Know the story and practice telling it, refining it through telling and letting it grow as the people you tell it to join in and let it become their story too.

And We Conclude?

> *Gain all you can, by common sense, by using in your business all the understanding which God has given you. It is amazing to observe, how few do this; how men run on in the same dull track with their forefathers. But whatever they do who know not God, this is no rule for you. It is a shame for a Christian not to improve upon them, in whatever he takes in hand. You should be continually learning, from the experience of others, or from your own experience, reading, and reflection, to do everything you have to do better to-day than you did yesterday. And see that you practise whatever you learn, that you may make the best of all that is in your hands.*

> Good advice from John Wesley! This comes from his sermon on money. Christians take note; knowing God will help you to be innovative, so ask Him for advice every step of the way.

We've covered a lot of ground business-wise. Hopefully you feel equipped for life as an entrepreneur! But what was promised to you was a mission strategy, a way to change the world. Why is business such a good mission vehicle? Well it can directly bring about social and environmental transformation, it can provide employment and generate wealth to be shared. But another reason why business can be used for God as well as for good is because of the network of contacts it generates. From employees and their families, to suppliers to customers, actually business is all about people. And so is the Kingdom!

And We Conclude FINALLY

> *So neither the one who plants nor the one who waters is anything, but only God, who makes things grow. The one who plants and the one who waters have one purpose, and they will each be rewarded according to their own labour. For we are co-workers in God's service; you are God's field, God's building. By the grace God has given me, I laid a foundation as a wise builder, and someone else is building on it. But each one should build with care. For no one can lay any foundation other than the one already laid, which is Jesus Christ. If anyone builds on this foundation using gold, silver, costly stones, wood, hay or straw, their work will be shown for what it is, because the Day will bring it to light. It will be revealed with fire, and the fire will test the quality of each person's work. If what has been built survives, the builder will receive a reward. If it is burned up, the builder will suffer loss but yet will be saved—even though only as one escaping through the flames.* 1 Corinthians 3:7–15

We have reached the end. We've told you what we know, we've told you what we think. Hopefully we have encouraged you to think that you can help to build the Kingdom through business. Now it's over to you. Is God calling you, your group or your church into one of His entrepreneurial enterprises?

There are several definitions of an entrepreneur, but the one that I like best is 'one who takes a risk in order to create something out of nothing'. Using this definition, God is the ultimate entrepreneur!

By all definitions entrepreneurs are risk takers. Good. Because it seems to me that as Christians we are called to be risk takers. Not risks for the thrill of it. Not blind risks, where we haven't calculated the cost. But risks in order to get whatever Jesus calls us to do done (which might end up being both thrilling and costly!). It would be a shame if fear of the unknown led us to try to play it safe. Playing it safe is not a biblical concept. Can you name me one Bible hero who played it safe? Jonah tried to, and look what happened to him! And thank God Jesus didn't play it safe ('you carry on like that lad and they'll nail you to a cross...better tone it down a bit'). In fact Jesus told several stories specifically about not playing it safe. One of them we've already referred to. It's recorded in Matthew's Gospel, chapter 25 starting at verse 14. You know the story; a man was going on a journey and he called his servants and entrusted his wealth to them. He gave one five bags of gold, another two bags and another one bag, each according to his ability. Then he went on his journey. The man who had received five bags of gold went at once and put his money to work and gained five bags more. The one with two bags of gold did the same and gained two more. But the man who had received one bag went off, dug a hole in the ground and hid his master's money. And when the master came back he was not at all pleased with the one who had played it safe and buried the money! Read for yourself what happened to him.

For those of us in business, this parable is a powerful and challenging one. It's about growing and investing. If I want Jesus to say to me well done good and faithful slave, I need to take some risks with what He has given me in order to grow the Kingdom. In fact, if I follow His lead and His call in my business I will probably find that it is a risky route He is leading me on. But He will be with me. We will be on the front line together, building His Kingdom. And there is no better place to be!

What They are Saying about Business and the Kingdom

There are many groups working in this area. We've put some of them in a directory at the end of this book, because they may be useful to you. But we also asked them to write down what their vision and passion were. And we got some very interesting answers! Be inspired!

Dr David Landrum, Evangelical Alliance

Business needs God. It's a simple as that. Our history is writ large with evidence that, without a guiding morality, the business and industry that should benefit us all simply becomes 'my business'. Relativism reigns at the moment. And, as with politics and society, the way that we run our economy is in desperate need of moral leadership. The Kingdom of God provides us with a model of how things should be, and evangelicals have got a great track record in demonstrating the Kingdom in business for His glory and our healing.

Our most hurting and broken communities in the UK need Kingdom oriented businesses. When we talk about justice, restoration, and renewal of these communities, on the most practical level, alongside sharing the good news of Jesus Christ, we are talking about jobs and employment. If we want to see transformed lives, we need to see business as mission – and take a lead.

Ram Gidoomal CBE, Chair of Traidcraft

My dream is to see a world where businesses are run on biblical principles that ensure a fair deal for all; producers, suppliers, buyers, sellers, shareholders, consumers and indeed all stakeholders. Is this possible? I believe it is and Traidcraft plc is an example of just such a business. Our strategic plan, from fair to flourishing, affirms that we want to see: 'A world freed from the scandal of poverty, where trade is just and people and communities can flourish'.

I dream of a society where:

- justice is given to all, not just to a favoured few who have justice by power or by wealth.
- we protect the most vulnerable people – the unborn, and those who are at the end of their lives.
- people are brought into right relationships with each other.
- active compassion is exercised and practised – not just talked and written about.
- stewardship of resources is taken seriously. Ours is a greedy hemisphere. The facts are bald and simple. There is more than enough for all. But some of us want most of it for ourselves.
- people living in the two thirds world are empowered to set up their own businesses and play their part as full members of the global business community.

Jerry Marshall, General Manager of Transformational Business Network (TBN)

Part of extending God's Kingdom is fighting poverty and injustice. Extreme poverty is a scandal: over 3 billion people live on a daily income of less than we pay for a cup of coffee. Millions die each year from poverty related causes.

Material wealth ultimately comes from generating an income by adding value to customers' lives and private enterprise, for all its flaws, is the best way to do this. Small and medium enterprises (SMEs) are of particular value to developing countries. They have the potential for rapid employment growth, they encourage a spirit of enterprise and they bring positive pressure to improve the efficiency and transparency of the market and government. But most developing countries have relatively few SMEs, a 'missing middle'.

Transformational Business Network (TBN) is part of the solution. TBN is a Christian-based network of business and professional people who tackle poverty through business. Members encourage the development of SMEs through partnering with local entrepreneurs, mentoring, training, investment and accessing markets.

This is an outworking of our anointing for business and should be firmly rooted in the church. Entrepreneurs need to be part of a church accountability structure as we are often more exposed than most to the temptations of the world. And the Church needs to move beyond seeing business merely as a source of funds and venue for evangelism and welcome the apostolic gifting of enterprise and risk into their leadership mix.

Transformational SME: Transforming Lives Through Business

Transformational SME was created in the late 1990s with the goal of supporting the growth and development of Christian-owned and managed small-medium enterprise (SME) in the

Arab world and Asia. We are a global community of Christian investors, which as well as providing financial investment from our pooled resources to qualifying SMEs, add further value through mentoring, coaching and other forms of assistance. We provide mezzanine finance to companies operating in our target market after carefully reviewing their plans, performance and capabilities and aligning them against the criteria and objectives of the fund.

Transformational SME is led by an international team of business men and women with accumulated experience of more than 150 years in:

- venture capital and finance.
- entrepreneurship and management.
- international business and cross-cultural living in the Arab world and Asia.

Charles Hippsley: The London Institute for Contemporary Christianity

Founded on John Stott's principle of 'double listening' (an ear to the word and an ear to the world), the London Institute for Contemporary Christianity (LICC) has recognised the centrality of work in God's purposes since its inception some 30 years ago. LICC has championed the cause of whole life discipleship, and has developed and distributed a wide range of free and purchasable resources supporting Christians in the workplace and their church communities. Visit our website to access these.

Within this context, we see BAM as a key way for Christians to participate in the Kingdom work of building good companies with godly values and an eye for the powerless in societies: providing much needed employment both in the UK and oversees. In 2012 we launched the LICC Work Forum, with a specific remit to drive forward a portfolio of workplace initiatives. One such, Executive Toolbox, is equipping a tranche of senior managers and entrepreneurs to have a transformational impact in and through their various enterprises. We are excited to hear reports of real transformation as the BAM movement grows and to participate in its development.

Terry Diggines: A Call to Business

I have a dream that our churches have an ethos that values, encourages, equips, releases and recognises all who are in the workplace as workplace ministers with a calling on their lives.

I have a dream that business owners understand there is a calling on their lives, and that their business is a ministry, and not just for 'the ministry'. And that there is a commitment to seek first the Kingdom of God and ensure this is reflected in the foundations and values of the company; this is key to the Kingdom of God being advanced through business.

I have a dream that those in employment acknowledge they are a ministers in the workplace, with a sense of calling, recognising their job as a ministry. And that they have an understanding that they are agents of change and transformation. As St Paul writes:

> *Whatever you do, work at with all of your heart, as working for the Lord, not for men since you know you will receive an inheritance from the Lord as a reward. It is the Lord Christ you are serving.* Colossians 3:23

I am called to business; I am a minister.

Bridget Adams: WorkPlace Inspired and the Kingdom Business School

We are passionate about the role of business in God's Kingdom plans and the sacred call to a life in business. We act as a focal point for Christians in business, and as an incubator for Kingdom businesses. WPI is based in The Hub, a Christian business community office space in Watford.

Running a KBB can be a lonely job; it's difficult for any of us to go it alone, even with God as our CEO. So we hope we can support and encourage those who are committed to building the Kingdom through business. And we like what happens when you put Kingdom businesses together; expansion seems to happen naturally through mutual collaboration and cross fertilisation!

Proverbs 31:10–31

A wife of noble character who can find?
She is worth far more than rubies.
Her husband has full confidence in her
and lacks nothing of value.
She brings him good, not harm,
all the days of her life.
She selects wool and flax
and works with eager hands.
She is like the merchant ships,
bringing her food from afar.
She gets up while it is still night;
she provides food for her family
and portions for her female servants.
She considers a field and buys it;
out of her earnings she plants a vineyard.
She sets about her work vigorously;
her arms are strong for her tasks.
She sees that her trading is profitable,
and her lamp does not go out at night.
In her hand she holds the distaff
and grasps the spindle with her fingers.
She opens her arms to the poor
and extends her hands to the needy.
When it snows, she has no fear for her household;
for all of them are clothed in scarlet.
She makes coverings for her bed;
she is clothed in fine linen and purple.
Her husband is respected at the city gate,
where he takes his seat among the elders of the land.

She makes linen garments and sells them,
and supplies the merchants with sashes.
She is clothed with strength and dignity;
she can laugh at the days to come.
She speaks with wisdom,
and faithful instruction is on her tongue.
She watches over the affairs of her household
and does not eat the bread of idleness.
Her children arise and call her blessed;
her husband also, and he praises her:
'Many women do noble things,
but you surpass them all.'
Charm is deceptive, and beauty is fleeting;
but a woman who fears the LORD is to be praised.
Honour her for all that her hands have done,
and let her works bring her praise at the city gate.

Resource Directory

A Call to Business; a growing community of business people who believe that God has called them into business not simply to work, but to influence and change the very environment of business in general and the City in particular, and to see many people come to faith in Jesus.

www.acalltobusiness.co.uk

BAM Global Think Tank; listen, learn, connect, share, invigorate

bamthinktank.org

Business as Mission; Business as Mission Resources; get fresh ideas, take new steps

www.businessasmission.com

CABE; affirming Christians in business

www.cabe-online.org

Forum for Change Business Cluster;

www.eauk.org/forumforchange/business.cfm

Instant Apostle; a publishing community for the 21st century

www.instantapostle.com

LICC; equipping Christians and churches for whole-life discipleship in the world

www.licc.org.uk

LightLunch; midweek Christian worship for London Business

www.africalinkup.com/lightlunch/index.html

Mats Tunehag
www.matstunehag.com/

South Asian Forum of the Evangelical Alliance; a forum for South Asian Christians in the UK to encourage, support and equip each other for mission, and to represent their concerns to Government, media and the wider Church.
www.eauk.org/saf

TBN; business solutions to poverty
www.tbnetwork.org

The Wheaton Declaration on Business as Integral Calling
www.businessaic.com

Traidcraft; fighting poverty through trade
www.traidcraft.co.uk/

Transformational SME; transforming lives through business
www.transformationalsme.org

UK Evangelical Alliance; uniting to change the world
www.eauk.org

WorkPlace Inspired and the Kingdom Business School; building the Kingdom in and through business
www.workplaceinspired.com

Some Books We Found Helpful

Brafman, O. and Beckstrom, R.A. *The Starfish and the Spider; the unstoppable power of leaderless organisations* (New York: Penguin Group, 2006)

Branson, R. *Screw Business as Usual* (London: Virgin Books, 2011)

Buckingham, M. and Clifton D. O. *Now Discover your Strengths* (London: Pocket Books, 2005)

Carrette, J. and R. King, *Selling Spirituality; the Silent Takeover of Religion* (Abingdon: Routledge, 2005)

Cosden, D. *The Heavenly Good of Earthly Work* (Bletchley: Paternoster, 2006)

Costa, K. *God at Work* (London: Continuum, 2007)

Featherby, J. *The White Swan Formula* (London: LICC, 2009)

Greene, M. *Thank God it's Monday; Ministry in the Workplace* (Bletchley: Scripture Union, 1997 edition)

Grundy, M. *An Unholy Conspiracy; the scandal of the separation of Church and Industry since the Reformation* (Norwich: The Canterbury Press Norwich, 1992)

Handy, C. *The Empty Raincoat; Making Sense of the Future* (London: Random House UK, 1994)

Handy, C. *The Hungry Spirit* (London: Arrow, 2002)

Heslam, P. *Transforming Capitalism* (Cambridge: Grove Books, 2010)

Lambert, S. *A Book of Sparks* (Watford: Instant Apostle, 2012)

Pearson, G. *Towards the Conversion of England; a Report Revisited* (Cambridge: Grove Books, 2005)

Vernon, A. *A Quaker Business Man; The Life of Joseph Rowntree* (York: Sessions Book Trust, 1987)

Windsor, D.B. *The Quaker Enterprise: Friends in Business* (London: Frederick Muller, 1980)